Brands,
Political
Brands,
and
Donald
Trump

By Jess M. Collen

Print edtion ISBN: 978-1-7359613-0-9
Ebook edition ISBN: 978-1-7359613-1-6

CONTENTS

INTRODUCTION

Is there a difference in politics between name recognition and branding? In my mind there is. Over the years, the distinction between name recognition and branding has not been given a lot of serious thought. When people hear the term *name recognition*, they usually picture voters lingering over a ballot, trying to summon what they know about the candidates. The idea is that voters will choose a name they recognize over one they do not, even if they know little to nothing about the candidate with the most familiar name.

Branding begins with name recognition, but it can go far beyond just recognition of a name. The branding process weaves many traits and characteristics into the meaning of the name. Branding will tell a story about a product—or candidate's—predictability, and sometimes will elicit an emotional attachment. Political name recognition often gives that voter only the illusion of familiarity; a political brand means that the voter knows, or feels, something about the candidate behind the name.

This is an introduction to the idea and concept of political brands, and the striking similarity of those brands to any other commercial product brand. This book is presented through a series of pieces I have previously published as a contributor to *Forbes* magazine. Each essay deals either with a political brand, or a fundamental truth related to commercial product brands and trademarks.

In some ways, America has never lived a moment like this, where the name brand of a political leader—President Donald J. Trump if you have not already guessed—has been so intricately intertwined with the ideas of product brand, entertainment personality, political leader, and most powerful person on planet Earth. Donald Trump was never the motivation for my book; the idea of comparing product brand to political brand germinated a long time before Mr. Trump ever ran a serious political campaign. The concept of brand names and politics has existed in American politics since long before the Continental Congress, and well before the Constitution. Nor are politician brands unique, by any means, to the United States of America.

But at this time of the 2020 Presidential election, with the critical date just weeks away, I thought it would be interesting to arrange some of what I have written over the years in Forbes into a story which shows how product brand names and political brands often combine. The experiences of many politicians, and of many name-brand products, merge together to help illustrate the impact of brand names and politics on President Donald Trump.

When you ask the average American voter to identify the most famous political brand names in our history, one of the leading responses is always "the Kennedys". On September 8, 2020, in the Massachusetts Democratic primary for United States Senate, Representative Joseph Kennedy lost the election to incumbent Sen. Edward Markey. Markey ended up winning by a comfortable margin of over ten points. Kennedy started the campaign as a heavy favorite. Since Kennedy's loss, the press, both at home in Massachusetts and elsewhere, has been proclaiming the death of the Kennedy dynasty. It was the first Kennedy loss ever in a statewide election in the Commonwealth of Massachusetts, and one of the only statewide electoral losses ever suffered by any Kennedy family member in *any* state. I was fortunate enough to track down an advisor to Sen. Markey and ask him his view on this. Here is what he said:

> Since Kennedy's loss, the press, both at home in Massachusetts and elsewhere, has been proclaiming the death of the Kennedy dynasty. Rep. Kennedy was the first Kennedy ever

to lose a statewide election in the Commonwealth of Massachusetts. The loss was one of the only statewide electoral losses ever suffered by any Kennedy family member in *any* state. This alone was headline news in Boston. The media site NBCBOSTON.com spoke for many when it concluded: Kennedy Loss in Massachusetts May Mark End of 'Camelot' Era (the phrase so often associated with an idyllic view of JFK's presidency, a place where legend said 'the rain must never fall 'till after sundown'). But others were less sanguine. Boston Globe columnist Scott Lehigh wrote an opinion piece entitled "JPK III didn't demolish the Kennedy dynasty—it faded long ago". He said that "nostalgia aside, the Kennedys haven't been a dynasty for decades".

The facts would seem to contradict this statement. I was fortunate enough to track down Scott Ferson, CEO of Liberty Square Group, a former press secretary for Senator Ted Kennedy, and a Markey strategist in the 2020 primary. Mr. Ferson was perhaps uniquely situated to understand what role the Kennedy name did—and did not—play in this election. Here is what he observed: "Market polling showed that people really liked Joe Kennedy". During the campaign, the legacy was attacked by some "fake news" and dirty tricks initiated by a tiny handful of social media accounts, mentioning infamous national events like the assassination, and Chappaquiddick (Sen. Kennedy's involvement with a fatal 1968 automobile accident). Ferson analyzed the impact of these attacks, saying that the Kennedy campaign's strategy to embrace its role of victim of this hate speech did not play well among voters. "But the loss was not a rejection of the Kennedys." The Kennedy brand still holds its allure. "We were in Brockton (Mass.) for a caucus, and Joe Kennedy packed them in. But Ed Markey took every delegate in the election. Kennedy was a celebrity and people love celebrities. But who they love is different from who they voted for."

Sometimes a great brand runs up against stiff competition in the marketplace. Losing an election—even for the first time in seventy years—does not mean a brand is dead. Even championship sports teams lose games on occasion. As Scott said of the Kennedys, "they were 26-1".

Political brand names, like any brand names, tend to die hard.

For almost any successful product, the brand is an important selling feature. But the brand is not the only reason for success. A product has to successfully solve the problem it is designed for: soap needs to clean well or smell nice, or both; running shoes should feel good on the feet and help a runner's gait; an HDTV must deliver a sharp picture and sound, and seamlessly stream content as well. A political brand will say: my history tells you that I stand up for the things that you find important. But I can also deliver on my promises; I can influence other people on your behalf and get the job done.

Product brands and political brands are far more alike than most people realize. In fact, they are exceptionally similar. As an intellectual property lawyer, I have had a 35-year career protecting, defending and enforcing rights in product brand names from around the world. Not only have I seen how brands touch consumers' imaginations and their rational brains, but I have seen in great detail what makes brands successful, and why they sometimes fail. I have been able to pinpoint what it is about similar product names—the touchstone issue for legal trademark infringement—that are so damaging when misused.

Following shortly on the heels of the November 2020 election will be my upcoming book, which will look in depth at political brands and at product brands, and all of the facts and reasons which combine to sometimes make people from political families more likely to succeed and more likely to get the job done when elected. Candidates benefiting from strong political brand names may in fact be superior candidates.

There is no doubt that star power, name power, or both, use a recognizable name to open the door to success, if, like any asset, the name is properly managed and deployed. And just like in the commercial marketplace for consumer products, negative brand association will cause a politician's brand to fail in politics.

Donald J. Trump was hardly the first brand name to enter politics, but he has been the only one to go from commercial product to the Presidency. Name recognition has always played an important role in electoral politics. Not everything that politicians typically refer to as "name recognition" is really what the commercial world calls "branding".

What has happened to the "TRUMP" brand name during the Trump presidency? Outwardly, it seems not to have flourished, though its renaissance may be just around the corner. It is not clear how much Donald Trump was actively orchestrating Trump businesses, or making businesses, since his inauguration on January 20, 2016. There was much discussion about what amount the "TRUMP" brand has benefited from the presidency, but much of this dissipated after the first year or two.

Trump achieved the highest office on the strength of his brand. Despite clashes within his own administration, including cabinet members, advisors and ambassadors, he and his loyal brand ambassadors pressed forward in support of his cause. The "TRUMP" brand was well established, as we will see below. Donald Trump owned many federal registrations for the "TRUMP" trademark, as do other members of his family. His love of branding all things "TRUMP" is legendary. The name Trump uniquely bridges the gap between traditional commercial brand, and political name recognition.

PART I

PRESIDENTIAL
BRANDS AND
POLITICAL
FAMILY NAMES

Introduction and Commentary

Everyone knows that the "Trump" brand name has always been paramount to the president and his business endeavors. As an aggressive trademark owner, Mr. Trump had his share of trademark litigation experiences. Still, there has been nothing particularly unique or distinctive about his pattern of enforcing his trademark rights, nor did his trademark ownership seem likely to skew his view on America's involvement in international trademark treaties to which the U.S. was a partner.

Examining Trump's History: The New President and Trademark Rights

Nov 10, 2016

What does Mr. Trump's history of trademark litigation foretell? We've made an extensive examination of lawsuits filed, administrative challenges in the Trademark Office, and Trump's history of trademark registration ownership.

Two of the things about Donald Trump, which have become legendary, are his love of the "Trump" brand and his love of litigation. What do his trademark lawsuits and registrations foretell about the course of trademark law in this country for the next four years?

Let's be honest. With healthcare, immigration, job creation, and nuclear codes among the things that the transition team must fix, trademarks are not exactly part of the first 100 days' agenda. As important a role as they play in today's connected economy, trademark policy is something candidates rarely (if ever) discuss. We're told that Mrs. Clinton was once herself an IP lawyer. But presidents have not traditionally been significant brand owners. Ford Motor Company did not come from Gerald. Vacuum cleaners were not made by Herbert. Taylor wines did not come from Zachary's family. Obamacare is from Barack, but that's different.

If the candidates in an election between a former IP lawyer and a king of brand names don't talk about trademarks in a campaign, no one ever will. This seems to be the case even the one time there is a significant public policy concern, namely, whether trademark registration may be refused or canceled when applied to arguably disparaging trademarks, such as "The Slants" or "Redskins." We're unlikely to see a role for trademark law issues more prominent in political discourse than that.

Mr. Trump has been a diligent trademark owner. Federal court records show that Donald J. Trump or some Trump company or organization has been involved in a half dozen federal trademark lawsuits over the past ten years. The most recent suit in 2015 technically was a false advertising matter, not a trademark case. His Las Vegas companies filed a case against two labor unions which had circulated a flyer stating that Mr. Trump did not stay at one of his own resorts during an early campaign stop in Nevada, but rather stayed at a competitor's property—a fact which he denies. The claim was that this allegedly false statement caused reputational injury to the Trump Hotel Las Vegas and constituted false advertising.

The lawsuit characterized Mr. Trump as *"...the archetypical businessman—a deal maker without peer. Mr. Trump is a world-famous individual, and his name is synonymous with fame, fortune, and luxury."* (The court dismissed the case this August, the Trump organization did not attempt to amend its papers, and agreed to the dismissal.)

Before that, the last case showing up under the trademark records in federal court went back to 2008 and involved a dispute over registration of the domain name for "Trump Plaza Of The Palm Beaches" by an independent broker. Pretty routine stuff. In all, there are about seventeen trademark cases over the past twenty-five years. None would give the sense Mr. Trump would favor either more robust infringement remedies in court or more liberal protections for alleged infringers.

Looking at litigation within the Trademark Office, which typically attempts to block registration to another party based on a claim of confusion, the Trump organization has been a bit more active. But the records do not reflect any activity that appears to be outside the norm of trademark action for the owner of so many marks. This type of trademark protection activity is not unusual for a portfolio of this size. When a mark often consists of a common term, like "trump," which also has multiple dictionary meanings, conflicts are pretty certain to arise.

The Trump organization owns a lot of marks. I've written for several years about the Trump marks and, more recently, of course, their political implications.[1]

In all, there are probably in excess of one hundred current existing federal registrations to Donald Trump and/or his companies. Sifting through the ownership records might be like what Mr. Trump warned us about those tax returns: it's complicated. This figure excludes the several marks owned by Melania and the large and growing stable of "Ivanka Trump" registrations for her products. It also excludes several political slogans and the large number of marks he formerly controlled in association with the beauty pageant businesses he sold last year, or from an Indiana casino operation which was undertaken over a decade ago.

Among trademark registrations, there is again no indication that Mr. Trump's company has any unique protection strategy. Clearly, the number of registrations is robust. One could arguably say that the President-elect is more active in the U.S. Patent and Trademark Office than might be necessary, seeking out registration for more uses than perhaps the average well-funded trademark owner. But upon

---

1   June 21, 2013—*Trump Comes To Vancouver: More Real Estate, 'CrowdFunding' And Another Run For President?* (page 33)

June 18, 2015—*Bush And Trump: How Big Brands In Politics Work Like Any Other Trademark*

February 5, 2016—*Can Trump Trademark Ted Cruz's 'Trumpertantrum'?* (page 85)

February 7, 2016—*Woman Says Ted Cruz Is A 'Liar And A Thief' For Stealing Credit For 'Trumpertantrum'* (page 89)

examining the many trademark registrations, there is no pattern that suggests a special view on what or how to register marks.

On the other hand, unlike almost any other president in history, Donald Trump has first-hand familiarity with the concept of marks and brands. He knows the time, money, and effort needed for their care and feeding.

As for trade legislation and trademarks? Certain features of NAFTA address trademark rights. If Mr. Trump goes after NAFTA as he has promised, there could be an impact on trademark laws. But the impact likely would be very minor. NAFTA certainly has not created any NAFTA-wide trademark rights. Trademark owners still must file separate applications to register marks here, in Canada, and Mexico. Even an evisceration of the NAFTA deal would not change much. Certain provisions prohibiting registration of "geographically misdescriptive" terms were inserted into our trademark law specifically as part of our membership in NAFTA. This legal issue comes up occasionally but is hardly front-page news. I participated, together with a panel of Canadian colleagues, in a seminar in Montreal in 1994, where we discussed how NAFTA would impact trademark law. The prediction at that time was not much. There were hopes and thoughts of more trade among the three partner nations, leading to more trademark registration efforts in each country as a by-product of more and freer trade. That came to pass.

We've long been a part of at least two other major treaties on Trademark law: the Paris Convention and the Madrid Protocol. Paris has been around for over a century, and there is nothing to suggest in any way that this will change. Madrid has been part of our law since 2003. It permits a sort of streamlined style for filing trademark applications in multiple jurisdictions. Multinational trademark owners were heavily in favor. In practice, there is nothing in this treaty that should catch the incoming administration's attention.

We will have a President who is hypersensitive to the value of brand names. Efforts by the courts, legislature, or government agencies to lessen those protections will not find a receptive audience in the White House. The incoming President may even argue that his success is built entirely on the fame of his marks. Will that matter?

Introduction and Commentary

Every president is a brand. For example, Bill Clinton is like a bar of Ivory Soap.

Perhaps many people will disagree with this premise. But think about both entities. The soap, and Former President Clinton, each in its own orbit, represent success to an almost unattainable level. This is an exploration of Political brands and their striking similarity to any other brands for commercial products.

As we traverse back and forth between some of the stories and backgrounds of contemporary politicians and the importance of fame or family in developing a political brand, we are also going to take a hard look at how product brand names develop and are protected. When there are differences, they seem pretty clear and generally obvious. But the traits that make a great product brand name sell a product, and the traits that help sell political candidates, are very often the same.

Most election years feature a number of political candidates who own a family legacy in politics. The fall of 2014 yielded a very good example, which is discussed in this piece from 2014, based upon some comments made by the former Chief of Staff for President George W. Bush, speculating on the prospects for the President's brother Jeb to win the 2016 Republican presidential nomination:

Why Andrew Card is Wrong About Political Families

Nov 25, 2014

This month's election results were good (but not perfect) for political families.

Many of the high-profile races in these elections featured prominent American political families.

Florida joined the nepotistic political party by sending Democrat Gwenn Graham to Congress, defeating incumbent Republican Steve Sutherland, representing Florida's Second Congressional District. Graham's father, Bob Graham, is the former Governor of Florida and a former U.S. Senator. She made no statement of her family's political heritage in the election. Of course, one of the all-time American political families is also connected to Florida through leading politician, former governor, and perhaps future presidential candidate, Jeb Bush.

Jeb's son, George P. Bush, was elected as a land commissioner in Texas, apparently something of a unique Texas post, with a surprising amount of power and influence. It was his first crack at politics. A well-known name can get you a long way in politics, but $3 million (for a land commissioner campaign) does not hurt, either.

So why is Andrew Card, George W. Bush's Chief of Staff, saying Jeb would be a stronger candidate without the "Bush" brand? Andrew thinks that if Jeb ran under "John Ellis" (his given and middle names), he could sidestep all the baggage of the Bush name, and perhaps of any anti-dynasty bias (let's note that between Jeb and Hillary, someone's dynasty is going to be represented in 2016).

Sorry, Andrew, but there is little chance Jeb would be sitting where he is without having played the name card (sorry, Andrew). Regardless of his abilities and intelligence, Jeb may never have been able to capture the voters' attention if he did not share the name of two Presidents and have both father and brother in the White House. Moreover, voters' imaginations would not be as tickled by John Ellis of Florida as they are by the idea of a Bush in the White House again. No, GHWB and GWB were not always the people's choice. But the idea that Jeb could the skills and experiences of twelve years on Pennsylvania Avenue makes him an instant candidate, whenever he wants.

How did other political families fare this year?

The State of Georgia may have joined in on the Republican sweep, but they did so at the expense of political legacies. Sam Nunn's daughter lost on the Democratic ticket to the Republican "red tide" against a candidate named David Perdue. His first cousin, Sonny Perdue, is a former Georgia governor. Jason Carter, the grandson of former President Jimmy Carter, was pushed back by incumbent Governor Nathan Deal. Carter is a State Senator.

In Connecticut, Ted Kennedy Junior (running as a Democrat—sorry for the redundancy) won his first electoral bid in a statewide election in his home state of Connecticut, beating his Republican challenger named Bruce Wilson Junior from Connecticut's 12th District.

Mary Landrieu survived a tough challenge and is on to the December runoff in the State of Louisiana, though her prospects seem a bit dim.

Political son Andrew Cuomo was re-elected as Governor of the Empire State (he, like seemingly everyone else, also has ties to the Kennedy family).

The great State of Nevada sent another Laxalt, in his first political try, to the office of state Attorney General. The Republican upset Democrat Ross Miller, the grandson of former Senator and then

Governor Paul Laxalt. His connections allowed him to call on the likes of Mitt Romney, former Vice President Dick Cheney, and former United Nations Ambassador John Bolton. Oh, and before you go feeling sorry for Mr. Miller, having the misfortune of running against a political legacy, don't forget that Miller's father was also Governor of the State of Nevada.

In Hawaii, John Waihee won an at-large seat in the important Office of Hawaiian Affairs as a returning incumbent. The office is apparently a statewide government agency controlled by a group of trustees that control certain state lands (pursuant to a state constitutional provision). Waihee's father, John David Waihee, served for eight years as the Hawaii Governor.

It is hard to tell whether Mitch McConnell's rival in Kentucky, Alison Lundergan Grimes, who is currently Secretary of State of the Commonwealth of Kentucky, was helped substantially by her own name. Her father, Jerry Lundergan, is a former Democratic chairman and state representative. Name recognition from a state representative cannot be bad; adding the name power and connections of state political party chairman is even better. How else would a Kentucky Secretary of State and 35-year-old Senate candidate get help on the campaign trail from the likes of Bill Clinton and Joe Biden? I suppose it didn't hurt that she was running against the highest-ranking Republican in the Senate.

Introduction and Commentary

At one time, it seemed that a Vice Presidency and two Governorships would lead the Bush Dynasty to add an unprecedented third President to its legacy. The talk of the Bush legacy loomed large over Jeb Bush's presidential candidacy in the election of 2016:

Is the Bush Name a More Important Legacy than the Bush Library?

Apr 25, 2013

While the cameras are focused on George W. Bush in Dallas today, the big question is not the legacy of his papers, but what happens next to his name?

What next for the name "President Bush?" Barbara Bush (grandmother, not granddaughter) has just gone on record to say that the country does not need more Bushes in the White House. And despite Jeb Bush's silence on whether he would be a candidate, the allure of a call to run and the hard currency of a famous name could be too much to resist. Barbara Bush was quoted today as saying Jeb would get "half of our friends, and all of our enemies" if he runs. I am in no position to challenge the political wisdom of Barbara Bush. But I do know a few things about names, and about names in politics, and what I know is: (a) brand names sell in politics, and (b) like in showbiz, it may not matter what you say as long as they spell your name right.

The Presidents Bush have been informally distinguished as "41" and "43," or as "George H.W. Bush" and "George W. Bush." You have to wonder if Bush 41 resents having his name changed to accommodate this need to distinguish between them. During his public life, he was never known as George H.W. Bush. Yes, I think we did know (from the inaugural swearings-in) that he was George Herbert Walker Bush. But he was never George H.W. Bush. I suppose it's exactly what happens when a person names his son after him as a "junior." Sometimes, the elder then creates a new identity by referring to himself as "Senior." No matter. In the case of "President Bush," we need to know who's who.

We have a long, long history of political families and political family dynasties in this country. No hereditary political office is established under our Constitution, but the importance of a family name is strong as ever. Jeb Bush has made his own way with success as a big state governor. But there are lots of big state governors around, and not all of them are seen as presidential material. Jeb Bush is qualified, partly because he's Jeb, and partly because he's a Bush. The Bush name will stir up a melting pot of emotions to the American voter. Just like the name of any product, "Bush" evokes many different and even contradictory traits. Names do that.

To some, the main image will be a post-9/11 leader. To some, economic calamity. Some will recall "No Child Left Behind." Some will think of the Patriot Act. Others will think of the Gulf war victory under "41." But almost everyone will think "presidential." The focus may be on policy, but the "Bush" name says *President*. It's almost as much a part of the name as "George." *President Bush*.

Political families mean much more than name recognition, hard though it is to minimize the importance of the political brand name. Political families mean connections. And they mean growing up in an environment permeated by political talks, casual discussion with national and world leaders, and nurturing an ability to be comfortable in the presence of power and influence. Procter & Gamble may have an abundance of famous brands, but when they want to launch a new one, yes, it stands on its own. But the fact that P&G is behind it, with its savvy, skill, history, and credibility, all greatly increases the chances of success. Product names and political names are not that different.

If Jeb Bush decides to throw his hat into the ring someday, make no mistake about the importance of the *Bush* name in booting his candidacy to the top of the Republican leader board.

Is there a possibility that we could have another Bush-Clinton election in 2016? If the Bush name delivers gravitas to Jeb Bush, what does the Clinton name do for Hillary? She's already been a candidate. She won respect as Secretary of State. She has been in the public eye as an elected or appointed official for well over a decade. Perhaps, like Jeb Bush, her first election had to have been bolstered by her name. Unlike the Bush father/sons, the Clintons (Hillary and Bill) were always seen as a team. Maybe one with more dysfunction than the 2012 Red Sox, but a team still. Does that mean the "President Clinton" label helps her more than Jeb Bush? Or are there traditional— maybe even subliminal—mindsets in our society that make "branding" of the presidential office more readily transferred from father to son than from husband to wife?

It would be the biggest political brand showdown in American Presidential politics since former President Teddy Roosevelt came back to challenge sitting President Taft in the election of 1912 (they both lost to Woodrow Wilson). Former first lady Barbara Bush says, "we've had enough Bushes" in the White House. It will be interesting to see if her son Jeb can pass up a chance to capitalize on the brand value in the Bush name. That name legacy may be far larger than all of the documents, stone, and metal that we are seeing on the SMU campus today.

PART II

TRADEMARKS AND POLITICAL NAMES:
WHAT ARE THE GROUND RULES?

Introduction and Commentary

Let's look at some of the fundamentals of trademarks. These apply, as we said, to political families just as they do to products. But as a reminder of what a trademark is and how trademarks work, consider the following:

Eight Myths your Trademark Lawyer Should Dispel

Jan 9, 2015

Economists tell us we need more skilled engineers, researchers, and nurse practitioners. But one thing we have in abundance is capable trademark lawyers, meaning there's a pretty good chance the trademark lawyer you've hired has a depth of knowledge that will help you protect yourself and your brand.

Here are some key myths your lawyer in 2015 should be able to dispel:

1. *You Have To Get Your Trademark Registered.*

   Trademark registration is really valuable, but don't even try to get registration if your mark might be too similar to someone else's registration or might describe your product. You're asking for trouble.

2. *I Can't Get A Trademark Registration—I Don't Have A Logo.*

   Logos can be registered, but so can words alone, or designs, or smells, or sounds, or container shapes, and sometimes domain names, hashtags, or even colors.

   Hundreds of thousands of trademark applications, covering literally millions of products and services, are filed in the United States every year. Brand names are more important today to the U.S. economy than they were ten years ago.

3. *If Your Trademark Application Gets Opposed by a Big Company, You Should Just Give Up.*

Not true. Many big companies have thousands—or tens of thousands—of trademarks all over the world which they must police. If there's an easy way to find a solution, many sophisticated trademark owners are anxious to talk. Of course, companies are as different as people, with different corporate personalities and philosophies. But major trademark owners are often very pragmatic and responsible corporate citizens and, frankly, may not be all that concerned about your trademark if you are open to working with them.

4. *You Can Get an International Registration For Your Trademark.*

OK, this one is technically true but practically false. There is such a thing as an "international registration," but it is really no more than an international application that makes it easier for you to seek registration in countries around the world. Don't be fooled.

5. *If Someone Infringes Your Trademark, You Can Sue For Damages And Attorneys Fees.*

Again, true, but it's a myth that Trademark infringement litigation is almost ever a moneymaking proposition after you pay for your own lawyer. Precious few parties in trademark infringement lawsuits ever qualify for attorneys' fees, and even damages are notoriously difficult to get.

6. *A Cutesy Spelling Will Make Your Mark Distinctive.*

Wrong again. Whether you spell "Kool" with a "K" or a "C," the words are going to sound the same.

7. *They Can't Touch Me—I Own A Federal Registration.*

Definitely untrue. Federal registration creates several legal "presumptions" about your trademark and your right to use the trademark. But it is far from bulletproof. In fact, in the first five years after registration, anyone can challenge your trademark registration for almost any reason they could have used to block your trademark application from becoming registered. Further, if a party used its mark before you did, they can stop you even if you have a registration, and they have none.

8. *Most Marks Are Going To End Up In A Conflict Somewhere Along The Line.*

False. Statistics tell us that most trademarks are going to live care-free lives.

Introduction and Commentary

Some of the world's most famous trademarks have become successful names for products and services, even when as trademarks they are not very good, and hard to protect, often because the terms are not distinctive and have been used by others in the past for the same, or at least a similar product. With almost any trademark, abundant fame will make it protectable. But adopting a weak mark at the beginning can often lead to failure. Here is a weak name that ended up doing okay for itself:

FACEBOOK was Born a Lousy Trademark

Feb 15, 2012

Would Facebook, by any other name, have been such a success? The financial community these days is all atwitter (sorry) about Facebook and its impending IPO. If I had been their trademark lawyer when the company was launched, I would have told them to find a different name. There are at least three lessons to be learned here: (1) the lesson of why FACEBOOK is not a good trademark for what they do; (2) the fact that I may not be graced with the greatest foresight; and (3) why and when (1) [and (2)] eventually do not matter to a company.

First and most importantly, why would this have been a bad trademark at the time Facebook started? A "facebook" is a name that had been used, either formally or informally, by students for a long time. When my oldest daughter started college in 2002, the freshman students, like generations before them, clung to the freshman register. You remember these. The freshman register was like a yearbook in reverse. It was filled with pictures of strangers who were your new classmates, not your departing friends. The book allowed you to put a name (and maybe a hometown and major) to a face. We had them when I was in college. Some people never looked at them while others seemed obsessed. In my daughter's college, they called it the "stalker book." This was literally an "offline" Facebook.

As everyone who has seen "The Social Network" remembers, they originally called it "The Facebook." When you decide what to call your company or product, your trademark lawyer is going to try to persuade you not to come up with a descriptive word. Descriptive words are tempting because they give you a jump start, telling the customer or user what your product is all about. But when you settle upon an ordinary descriptive term out of the everyday language, you are not going to be able to legally stop others from using the same name. There is a very good chance that some other entity calling itself "The College Facebook" could have happily used that name back in the day, and there's nothing that Zuckerberg and Co. could have done about it.

Contrast this with an arbitrary word like "APPLE" to sell computers. Now we're talking. Use a name like APPLE, which has nothing to do with the product or its user, and you are on the road to developing a very strong trademark that no one else can use in your market segment.

What Facebook has going for it now is the benefit of time. No place does time heal all wounds better than in trademark law. The longer a word has been in use, the stronger the owner's rights. So, over time (there's a typical presumption of five years in the law, but that is just a benchmark), an owner can have acquired exclusive rights even in a descriptive term. When Facebook launched in 2004, the word Facebook was a bad name. If you said Facebook to someone, they would have thought of one of those freshman directories. Today, of course, the word Facebook means the colossal global social networking (and much more) site. Over time, the company has earned rights to its name.

Maybe if it wasn't called Facebook, enough people wouldn't have known what it was, and the concept would never have taken off. But, that's doubtful. Look at examples all over the Internet. Google and Yahoo seem to do okay.

How many times have I told a client not to use a name, and they ignored me, and the product went on to be a hit? It would be a safe bet to say I am usually the big loser in the weekly office football pool, so gambling does not usually work so well for me. But winning with a descriptive trademark is a gamble. If you survive those early years, all is good. But, those early years are always the hardest to survive. Don't fall in love with your name, and don't take a name that you can't stop other people from using.

Sure, today, we can't imagine Facebook not being Facebook. Does that mean it was a good name? I don't think so. Even today, there are trademark disputes going on between Facebook and other companies. Facebook has even given up one of its earliest trademark registrations, which described its services as "providing an online directory information service featuring information regarding, and in the nature of, collegiate life, classifieds, virtual community, and social networking." (U.S. Trademark Registration No. 3,122,052.) And of course, by now, Facebook has just a few extra bucks they can spend on lawyers that may not have been so easy for them to spare in 2004.

If you're developing a product or a service that you expect within, say, the next decade or so, to yield you 845 million (and growing) consumers, then go for it. I don't know what the discussions were when they selected the name Facebook. It does appear that they filed a trademark application fairly soon after the site launched in full. For most companies, big, small, and medium, it's a really good idea to take a name that won't bog you down in challenges, litigation, and disputes. Descriptive names are the easy way out, and things don't always end up quite as well as they have for Facebook.

What does that say about the trademark lawyer? Well, in my own defense, I think I would have been right. Facebook has become a phenomenon of unmatched scope. There used to be an old saying: "Do the clothes make the man or does the man make the clothes?" It's the same with trademarks. Does a good name make a product? By the way, even though, personally, I recoil at the whole "my-everything" name trend, I would have been much happier approving the MYS-PACE trademark for a social network.

Introduction and Commentary

The pre-Presidential "Trump" brand has not been limited to the United States. If anything, the correlation between Trump and the perception of its total success in America (from business to entertainment to politics) makes it appear that the "Trump" brand is just taking a hiatus from the business while it runs the presidency for a while. This projects a desirable brand image to some consumers of "Trump" in other countries:

Trump Comes to Vancouver: More Real Estate, 'CrowdFunding' and Another Run for President?

Jun 21, 2013

Trump. Whether you love him or want to leave him on a porch swing somewhere, the name seems to sell real estate. For years, Donald Trump has been licensing his name to real estate developers around the world. The results have paid off handsomely. Yesterday, his latest venture, this one in Canada, was announced.

As if another 60-story skyscraper was not enough to heighten his ego, reports crop up about another run for the White House. How far can a name take you?

Wednesday's *Wall Street Journal* points out that no new U.S. development project has used the "Trump" brand name since 2007. But that is because the name has been going on the road. The Journal reports that the "Trump" name has been licensed to developers in Brazil, the Caucasus, Turkey, and has opened an office Shanghai. Whether and how much real estate development enterprises cross national boundaries, with different national laws, I can't say. It would seem like it would generally be only the rare commercial or residential property that was appealing because of the name over the door, as opposed to where the door is and what you find when you step inside (excluding hospitality industries, for instance). Does the Trump name sell overseas because it stands for Trump, or is it a sign of progress (and, dare I say, American-style), in the way that, to my tour guide in Shenzhen, China in 1992, the most prized construction in town was the new *McDonalds* that was going to open up in his city?

Then, there is the absence of the warts-and-all magnifier that may be present here in the USA. Having survived his share of financial troubles at home, the brand can be tainted in the eyes of some. But overseas, Trump may have a more unblemished appearance.

While the "Trump" mark has been registered in the United States for years, its presence abroad is generally more recent but surprisingly extensive. "Trump" is registered in Europe, Australia, South Korea, Philippines, Taiwan, New Zealand, Canada, the UK and Singapore. In all, counting "Trump" and various permutations such as "Trump Tower," "Trump World" (and don't forget about the "Donald J Trump Signature Collection"), there are well over 50 foreign registrations of the mark.

And if you like Trump's *Celebrity Apprentice*, how about "Celebrity Crowdfunding"? A hot thing in angle investment. Almost. Technically speaking, "crowdfunding" is not yet an investment. It's a donation for which you may receive something, just not an equity stake. At present, you must be an "accredited investor," with a minimum net worth of more than $1 million (exclusive of the value of one's primary residence) to be solicited to invest in a startup. But that's about to change. The JOBS (Jumpstart Our Business Startups) Act, enacted by Congress last year, will enable anyone to invest via equity crowdfunding sites. The JOBS Act is just awaiting SEC regulations to go into effect.

Trump launched FundAnything with the help of LearningAnnex founder Bill Zanker, a guy who knows a couple of things about mass appeal. FundAnything enables entrepreneurs to fund anything, from philanthropic campaigns to entrepreneurial initiatives. In a signature move to remain the center of attention, The Donald promises that, "I'm giving away money," and the site goes on to say that he will actually invest in some projects himself. There aren't any details on that point.

FundAnything has positioned itself to go head to head with crowdfunding stalwarts Indiegogo and Kickstarter. FundAnything feels the same and looks the same. What's the difference? According to Donald, it's The Donald. As he told Forbes, "Those other sites don't have Trump, and that's a big difference. They just don't have Trump." Bill Zanker had more to say: "Bringing Donald Trump into this changes the whole paradigm. It's totally different. For now, it's always been these Brooklyn hipsters doing it. Nobody knows about crowd-funding yet. You bring Donald into it, he's the most luxurious busi-nessman brand out there. It's a whole game changer."

Has anyone ever had more confidence in the value of a name—his own name?

A great developer no longer needs to know how to sweet talk zoning boards and spot value properties, or manage construction or even aesthetics. Give them the name, and let them build the product under it. How well does that concept work in Washington? I'm afraid we all think we know the answer to that one.

Introduction and Commentary

Some politicians are not satisfied with simply using their names. They also pursue registration of their names as trademarks in the United States Patent and Trademark Office. Such was the case with the former governor of Wisconsin, Scott Walker, and another familiar political brand, **Trump:**

Being Number One in Trademarks Owned Didn't Save Scott Walker; Donald Trump is Number Two

Sep 21, 2015

There are at least five new trademark applications filed for "Trump" since April alone, using Trump in some political way.

Governor Walker had quite a portfolio going. Some are the predictable: "Scott Walker For America" and "Walker16." A couple of his trademark applications are more message-laden, like "Reform. Growth. Safety." Then again, like many more pedestrian trademark applications, there are snags in the Trademark Office. It seems there is a clothing brand called "Duggie Scott Walker," which in the eyes of the Trademark Office, is going to prevent the Walker campaign from registering their trademark for t-shirts. They also question whether it is appropriate to grant trademark registration for using "Scott Walker For President" on printed material supporting the candidacy of Scott Walker for president. The Trademark Office feels, at least preliminarily, that this is not really a trademark but just a factual statement. This is also common fodder with in the Trademark Office's examination process.

As to Trump, maybe surprising, maybe not, only one of these five is owned by Donald Trump himself. The other four may just be people who are either his supporters, or are trying to profit from the

Trump phenomenon (which I guess would be appropriate), or a little of both.

On August 13, Mr. Trump filed a trademark application with the U.S. Patent and Trademark Office for the mark "Trump" for:

- Bumper stickers; decorative decals for vehicle windows; stickers; advertising signs of papers; advertising signs of cardboard; placards and banners of paper or cardboard; printed publications, namely, pamphlets providing information regarding Donald J. Trump as a political candidate; posters; pens.

- Clothing, namely, hats, sweatshirts, t-shirts, tank tops, headwear, long sleeve shirts; baby clothing, namely, one piece garments; children's clothing, namely, t-shirts.

- Campaign buttons.

- Political campaign services, namely, promoting public awareness of Donald J. Trump as a candidate for public office; providing online information regarding political issues and the 2016 presidential election; retail services in connection with political campaign goods.

- Political campaign services, namely, fundraising in the field of politics.

- On-line journals, namely, blogs featuring information about Donald J. Trump, namely, as it relates to politics and political campaigning; providing a website featuring non-downloadable videos and photographs in the field of politics and political campaigning; providing a website that features Donald J. Trump's views on political issues.

- Online social networking services in the field of politics and political campaigning provided via a website.

Pretty standard stuff. The application is pending in the Trademark Office, and was just assigned to one of the Trademark Office's attorneys for examination on Friday.

But who else is hoping to protect "Trump," the Trademark?

"Lady And The Trump." "Get Your Trump On," and "Americas Trump Card." "Trump Start America." "Trump: The Best Card In The Deck." Clever.

Then there are the more "red-meat" politician applications: "Trump This 2016," "Elect Trump Fire Washington," and "I Stump For Trump."

One application was filed to support "Ben Carson For President 2016."

If Governor Bush has been rehearsing for this job for a lifetime, he's not been very aggressive in the Trademark Office when it comes to seeking registrations. Once, his campaign in Florida owned registration for "JEB!" And now, a company called BHAG LLC has filed for "JEB!" for a whole shopping cart full of goods and services. "Mother Jones" reported early in the summer that this "mysterious" holding company is formed from the acronym for "Big Hairy Audacious Goals," which they say is a concept adopted by Mr. Bush.

Other than those, and Rand Paul's "Stand With Rand," there have been no great contenders for trademark primacy. Lest you think that the mark "Chris & Christy" was related to the New Jersey governor, this trademark application could be considered a "Gangnam-style" mark for leather goods and clothing, as it was owned by Sejung & Future Co., Ltd., a corporation of the Republic of Korea, at 962-1, Daechi-Dong, Gangnam-Gu, Seoul, Republic of Korea. (This application is no longer active.)

The Democrats are in a similar state. Mrs. Clinton is related to several marks owned by the Clinton Foundation of New York, but there are no campaign-related registrations, and nothing at all for Bernie Sanders or Joe Biden. Same story for Martin O'Malley and Lincoln Chaffee. Lawrence Lessig is a well-known scholar and law professor, with wide writings on copyright law, particularly on the Internet, and whose writings have also included trademark law issues. He has no applications either.

None of this is to suggest that trademark applications should be mandatory or are even "best practices" for presidential candidates. But it is certainly consistent that the Trump political brand has been well-documented on the commercial side as well, both by Mr. Trump and by others. And not every phrase can stick like "I Like Ike" or "All The Way With LBJ

Introduction and Commentary

It is also important to keep in mind that anything that identifies a product can be a trademark. It does not have to be just words. A famous label? See how **Jack Daniels** went after an imitator:

Trademark Lessons Pour from the Jack Daniel's Whiskey Bottle

Apr 25, 2018

Maybe you have just read that Jack Daniel's whiskey has sued a company in Texas for trademark infringement. The company sells the brand "Lonehand," with nary a "Jack" or "Daniel's" to be found on its label. But this suit provides an outstanding lesson how a company can claim trademark protection for packaging. It also draws a roadmap for the types of things to avoid if your startup's product might be targeting a market long dominated by another company. This is about the bottle and the label, not about the name.

Jack Daniel's starts out by describing its product as one of the "oldest, longest-selling and most iconic consumer products in American history." Talk about setting a high bar for yourself.

I think businesspeople generally know that legal prohibitions against copying trademarks are not limited just to words, names, or logos, but can also extend to other things like packaging, labeling, or anything else that may confuse consumers. In this lawsuit, Jack Daniel's starts off by pointing out that it owns federal registration for its "square bottle container." It also owns a registration for the label design which uses "Jack Daniel's" in a certain script and configuration, combined with other wording such as "Old No. 7" and "Tennessee Whiskey." It objects to Lonehand's use of a square bottle with "angled shoulders, beveled corners and a ribbed neck." The claim that Lonehand's written "arched lettering" is also confusing with Jack Daniel's label.

But wait, there's more. Jack Daniels alleges that Lonehand's marketing strategy employs the age-old trick (my description, not theirs) to have retailers display their product adjacent to Jack Daniel's, and to use white on black lettering reminiscent of the Jack Daniel's label.

Further still, owners of a very strong trademark can expand their litigation complaints beyond just the question of whether consumers will be confused. They can claim that someone else's use of a mark might reduce or "dilute" the value of their distinctiveness, built up over years and often decades. Here, Jack Daniel's cites critical customer reviews of the Lonehand product, calling Lonehand "the worst whiskey or bourbon I have ever had," and describing Lonehand's "weird aftertaste," or even calling it "swill compared to Jack Daniel's." They claim this association is damaging their mark.

Online consumer complaints are far from enough to prove a case. People's opinions are posted everywhere, and the fact that someone may not like a product or may not find it to be of a comparable quality does not necessarily mean it is unlawful to sell. Everyone is familiar with the fact that the range of quality for virtually any product is a broad one. (One of the reviews that Jack Daniel's puts in its lawsuit talks about quality in terms of pogo sticks vs. BMWs.) But you are always free to make a cheaper, and even lower quality, product. The law allows and tries to encourage all fair competition. When there is a claim of trademark infringement, the court may weigh a factor like bad online reviews, but it is only one of very many considerations. The voices of random consumer opinions do not necessarily carry great weight, especially since no one really knows who these people are, and what their background or prejudices are.

Of course, the California court is going to have to decide whether it believes essentially that consumers are confused that this other product is produced by or somehow affiliated with Jack Daniel's, or alternatively that the Jack Daniel's mark is so strong that the Lonehand product either tarnishes Jack Daniel's reputation, or blurs the line between Jack Daniel's as the source of these products and some other company.

Does this mean you cannot come out with a competitive product and use a similar package? Certainly not; any stroll through your neighborhood supermarket, drugstore or warehouse club proves that look-alike products are everywhere, and are thriving. (Totally as an aside, I have always thought that trademark owners could have aggressively stopped this practice 40 years ago if they had attacked properly; but I digress.) But if you are thinking of selling a product which targets a major national brand, be aware that there is a lot more that is protectable than just the name. Jack Daniel's claims that over the years it has spent hundreds of millions of dollars on advertising, and realized billions of dollars of sales. That probably makes for an extraordinarily strong brand, but at the end of the day they are still going to have to prove some harm to their own distinctiveness, or show confusion among consumers. Their in-house and outside lawyers are an experienced bunch, and undoubtedly ready to offer this proof.

In marketing, just like in the real world, aggressive tactics may lead to aggressive consequences like lawsuits. This very well structured civil complaint raises all of the above, and other facts. But at the end of the day, it is going to come down to a jury's opinion. If you look at the Lonehand bottle and the Jack Daniel's bottle, you cannot help but notice similarities. The jury is going to have to think about whether these similarities are going to confuse consumers. Maybe Lonehand will try to put on evidence that other whiskey or brown liquor products are sold in similarly shaped bottles, and maybe even with black labels, or black closures wrapped around the bottle cap. The safest advice for your new product is just to stay away from all of those features your competitor is using. But marketers have long since learned, and consumers have to some extent accepted the fact, that some lettering similarities and packaging similarities do not necessarily mean that the products come from the same source. Are consumers of this type of product sophisticated enough to recognize the difference?

Introduction and Commentary

While the focus here is principally on political trademarks, do not forget that a famous name can come from many fields. Entertainment is one of them. Donald Trump was, of course, both businessman and an entertainer, earning substantial sums for his role as a television mogul on The Apprentice. Famous names provide brand appeal for show business families as for politicians:

Andy Bernard Spills the Secret: What's in a Name— Fact or Fiction?

May 17, 2013

It's sort of like Andy Bernard's Freudian slip to Darryl in last night's finale of *The Office*. "Thanks, Dad, I mean Darryl." Parenting, or even the lack of parenting, makes an imprint. And it applies not only to personalities but sometimes to famous names.

The value of family names as trademarks is a topic that spans all endeavors, from business to politics, to sports and entertainment. Trademarks are packed with meaning. No less so family names, which indicate origin, qualities, traits, or talents. A product brand extension hopes to convince a customer that the new extension shares traits that consumers love about the original. Sometimes, the brand extension doesn't work.

Names in show business families can work in exactly the same way as product brand extensions. With people, the impact of the name is one of many factors in success. Just as with products, the brand is powerful. But not all-powerful.

I recently saw the premiere of an excellent new stage play called *Kunstler*, written by playwright Jeffrey Sweet. It is the story of the irascible and controversy-challenged activist/lawyer, William Kunstler, famous for many of his cases like the Attica prison riots and the Chicago 7. Later in his career, he was famous for defending high value, though arguably low moral, clients. Since I was not otherwise familiar with the playwright, I did a bit of research, and I found he had written a play in the 1980s called *The Value of Names*. The story builds upon an actress who wishes to change her family name in support of her career and the tension between whether she is changing her name to hide from her family or because the name helps her. The actress' father is a mostly retired famous actor. He thinks his daughter wants a name change, so she sounds less "ethnic" and not get turned down for certain parts. Since he named her, he tends to think that if any director does not want his daughter for certain parts, that might be a director's loss, not his daughter's. The daughter, on the other hand, doesn't want to get a part solely because of her father's famous last name. She wants to earn what she gets.

This one-act play does not really leave itself time to delve into whether the daughter believed that her family name would help her because people would think she inherited her father's talent, or learned at her father's hand, or even whether people might be inclined to hire her because they wanted to curry a favorable relationship with her famous father.

But *The Value of Names* has different facets. Show business names are like any other brand names. They convey meaning, and they imply a certain promise that the name will deliver upon. Is it a quality? Is it connections? Is it power? If the father was funny, will his daughter have his sense of humor? Ultimately, will audiences see her plays because her name brings a known quantity to the stage?

At one point in the play, the father refers to having had a small part in a play that featured an all-star cast full of well-known names. Usually, an "all-star" cast presumes the names will speak for themselves, and there is an assumption that the actors will deliver reliable, and to a degree, predictable performances. People don't want to see routine on screen or stage, but they do want to have a predictably good theater-going experience. The actors' names convey much.

The daughter in this play was worried that her name would convey too much. Regardless of her own talent, would she be hired for who her father was? Jane Fonda is an iconic Hollywood star. Would she have gotten her break if her father had not been a legendary Hollywood actor, Henry Fonda? Was it the connections, or was it the name, which was more valuable for helping her launch a career? For that matter, take Miley Cyrus. Her father, Billy Ray Cyrus, wasn't exactly the Henry Fonda of country-western, but he was a pretty well-known name who had at least one or two big hits. Did his name help her launch her career? Was it the name or the connections that helped her get started? Or did none of that matter in her case? Who knows? Certainly, her level of stardom far outstrips her father's.

The Office's Andy Bernard seemed to struggle to step outside his successful father's shadow. He probably would have loved a chance to get hired just because of his name.

PART III

SETTING THE STAGE:
GIVE ME A GOOD
BRAND NAME

Introduction and Commentary

It can be dangerous to abandon a venerable brand name for the sake of coming up with something new, different, and distinctive. Here is an example of one area where product brands and political brands are different. For a political brand name, a candidate is wedded to whatever name made them famous in their prior career as a business person, athlete, or entertainer. By comparison, in product branding—if nothing else—this decision by Kraft shows just how far consumer branding experts feel they need to go to create a different and distinctive moniker:

Mondelez? Puh-LEEZE!

Mar 21, 2012

Kraft just announced that it is going to rebrand its global snacks company Mondelez. According to their press release, we're supposed to say "mohn-dah-LEEZ." Easy to remember; just think Bush Administration Secretary of State. You know, Mon-de-leza Rice.

There are a couple of things that Kraft could do to spiff this up. One is to hyphenate it: Mon-delize. But you don't see the hyphen, and without that trick, it is hard to understand, sort of like hyperlipidemia. Or perhaps they could spell it differently, to give it more of flair, like Mon-deleez. But a word which needs to be explained and which can't be spoken without a pronunciation guide is not likely a word which the public is going to understand, let alone embrace.

It is not clear as of today whether Kraft has taken steps to protect this. One thing which happens with the world wide web and the round-the-clock news cycle is that often, the minute a new mark or name hits the public, some entrepreneur is off to the races, trying to lock up the term in the Trademark Office and with the local domain name registrar.

Remember the name BLUE IVY? Before the ink was dry on her birth certificate, someone had filed to register Beyoncé's baby name. No evidence of an "intent to use" trademark application is found for MONDELEZ in the official Trademark Office database; sometimes, there is a delay, so presumably, Kraft filed simultaneously with their announcement. Domain name registration is no clearer. Kraft does not own MONDELEZ.COM—someone else does. But perhaps they have acquired rights, or the owner is actually a related company or a proxy for Kraft. What this emphasizes, regardless of the actual facts, is that you have to coordinate naming efforts on many fronts. Once the name goes public, you have to assume that profiteers of all sorts want to share the benefits of your labors.

The domain name is generally first-come-first-served. The rules which govern domain name disputes do look at significant factors like intent in adopting a name, and it is possible to wrestle a name back if the owner happens to be a well-known domain name hoarder. If some individual happens to be the first to jump on the name, and they have no track record of commandeering other people's marks, you have to be prepared for a long, drawn-out battle, and resign yourself to the fact that the only way to get the name back is to pay for it.

From the Trademark Office's view, you must have a *bona fide* intention to use a mark before you qualify to file an application. Once you have filed, you need to complete use before you have any actual right to stop others. A mark filed in the Trademark Office by some third party who's trying to take advantage of hot news will create problems for the trademark owner since rights come only two ways: from prior use or prior filing. If there has yet to be use, the only way to lock in rights is to be the first to file. If you get beat in the foot-race to the Trademark Office, you then have to prove bad faith by the party which came before you. That can be very time consuming and expensive.

Kraft's press release reports that over 1,000 employees competed for the honor of branding the new company name. Kraft employees worldwide contributed over 1,700 choices. Apparently, two different employees each came up with MONDELEZ. What luck. Or maybe I should say "*what* luck"?

It is harder than ever to find a good name. (Obviously!) As more and more marks are registered with trademark offices and domain name registrars, finding a new name, conceptually an exciting pro-cess, becomes a chore. But sometimes you can just try too hard. The name has to speak to consumers and has to speak to investors (the very catchy MDLZ has already been locked in, say the reports). I do not think that Kraft is going to be getting an outpouring of praise for cooking up this new creation.

The shareholders still need to approve it, from what I understand. At least, for now, this is not a product name, just a company name. The new parent will mate its name to MONDELEZ CHIPS AHOY!, MONDELEZ OREO cookies, and MONDELEZ RITZ crackers. No MONDELEZA RICE crackers—at least not yet.

Introduction and Commentary

Still, the strongest of strong brands can afford to break the rules. "Starbucks" shortened its name from "Starbucks Coffee, Tea and Spice." "Apple" was born as "Apple Computer." And "Tesla" decided to ditch "Motors" from its company name:

Tesla Changes its Name:
Don't Try This at Home

Feb 1, 2017

Tesla shows that little things in a name can be *everything*. But trademarks are hard to establish and feed off a company's first accomplishments. Name changes—even small ones—have big implications.

Tesla announced that it is changing its name from Tesla Motors to Tesla. When they founded the company around the beginning of the century, the "motors" part of the name, no doubt, was critical. Perhaps they wanted to be seen as an alternative automobile company, and the founders no doubt liked the majesty of including the term "motors," like General Motors. Only big companies can make and sell cars, and adding Motors helped reinforce Tesla's place, and aspirations, in the industry.

Now, 13 years later, Tesla feels handcuffed by "motors" since it is finding other markets for the batteries it developed as part of its electric car business. With its solar-powered roof tile home battery systems from its acquisition of Solar City Corp, Tesla is more than cars. It seems like a natural to drop "motors," and besides, like with most marks, people tend to refer to the company by its first name, if the second part is a more descriptive term, like "motors." But if your mark is "General Motors," then you are unlikely to be referred to as "General," since "General" is, well, so general. I think of the scene in the 2000 movie *The Adventures of Rocky and Bullwinkle* (high-minded literary analogies are my stock-in-trade, and I don't mind repeating them) when a meeting takes place with several characters by the names General Admission, General Foods, and General Store.

Generally speaking, names like "general something" are about bigness, leaning on public recognition of General Foods (waning), General Motors, and General Mills, among others. If you want to sound big for certain products—or are at least targeting people old enough to remember when nothing connoted bigness like the phrase "who do they think they are, General Motors?"—even a term like "general" may have valuable connotations. (Before we write off General Motors' place as a cultural icon, we should note that they still own almost a thousand trademark registrations in the USA alone.)

But if your mark is a combination of a fairly uncommon term like Tesla, plus a common word like motors, people will shorten your name. If it is important for you to be always known by both names, you need to work like heck to consistently market yourself that way and be prepared to have to correct people, even customers. Otherwise, the free market of words will choose your moniker for you.

Tesla is hardly the first to drive down this road. Remember when Apple was Apple Computer? Did dropping "Computer" help it flourish in areas like music players and cell phones? Who can say? There could be something appealing about a company selling phones, which is a "computer" company. But from a pure trademark standpoint, Apple's decision seemed easy, since "computer" did not bring much to the dance.

Who remembers that Starbucks was once Starbucks Coffee, Tea and Spice? Or that Nintendo was preceded in time by the catchy Marufuku Co. Ltd. when it began life in the late 1800s, then Nintendo Playing Card Company? They changed to Nintendo a couple of generations ago. These changes were ultra-long term evolutions.

Note this type of name change is never without risk. Unless your business has recognition created by hundreds of millions or billions in value of combined advertising and free media coverage, dropping any part of your name may not be a winning proposition. If you have established a reputation for a single product, being chained to a name that suggests a more limited product offering does create issues. If you have success with one product under one name, and you want to leverage your name to a different product, will customers know for sure this is the same company they felt they already knew, or does even a small change cause consumers to worry if this is some different "Tesla" company? With Tesla, for the reasons already discussed, there may not be a big risk. But if you are not Tesla, think long and hard, and then long again, about whether there is more benefit to transferring your brand's goodwill to another product than tinkering with the name. The value of not only keeping your goodwill going but building on it, by expanding your portfolio, may well (and likely does) far outweigh the "comfort level" of being sure your name does not become misdescriptive of what you do.

Legally, the consequences become striking. What makes a mark strong is a combination of sales and advertising, which leads to consumer awareness. Even better is a mark that can be applied to not just one industry but to several. Then, even if an outsider in a third unrelated industry tries to adopt a mark similar to yours, you have the ability to argue, "yes we're known for SAAS, and yes we're also known for tax consulting, but our consumers certainly could think the people using our same mark for online ticket selling are us." Where a name spans more than one field, it is only reasonable that a consumer would think that businesses are related. This is not only logical; it is the way trademark law operates. Building goodwill is a compounding event, like interest. Plus, using the term "reasonable" in the law is always a good idea. It is the ultimate standard, so using the word makes everything you say sound more sophisticated.

Then there is the practical cost. Tesla Motors owns dozens of federal trademark registrations, and no doubt has an unmanageable number of other governmental filings. All of these have to be changed. The legal cost associated with a smaller enterprise's change is proportionally less, but still is a time and money zapper.

There are times when a name change is appropriate. Sometimes your product or service offerings will evolve or even pivot entirely to take away some or much of the appeal of the original name. But it is hard and costly work to nurture trademark rights. Those rights may be your most valuable asset. A new name may be able to springboard off of your original name if you are just dropping or changing one portion. But any change in your mark is creating a weak point that some potential competitor down the road can try to exploit against you. The strongest trademark rights are beneficiaries of progressive and perpetual care and feeding of the same mark. You compromise your rights by veering, even a little bit, into another lane.

Introduction and Commentary

Registering a trademark for a politician or anything else can be quite a challenge in the United States. On the other hand, registering an Internet domain name can be as simple as finding a name that no one has reserved yet. But trademark and domain name registration authorities are equal opportunity rejecters. Politicians cannot always get what they want. Even the Pope himself has to deal with this bureaucracy:

Trademark Issues for New Pope Francis?

Mar 12, 2013

Even a Pope has trademark issues. The Vatican owns trademarks, while there are rumors that the Pope Emeritus himself may be put to the test of trademark infringement.

When a new Pope is elected, he will also be responsible for a portfolio of trademarks. The Vatican is perhaps an unlikely trademark owner, but the owner it is. The marks are not necessarily catchy. For instance, "Benedictvs XVI Pontifex Maximus" was applied for virtually every product and service imaginable. Indeed there are others like "Ioannes Pavlvs Pontifex Maximus," "Stato Della Citta Del Vaticano" (State of Vatican City), and the ever-popular "Segreteria Di Stato" (Secretary of State). The owner is the Holy See and Vatican City.

There is a mystery about the Vatican's marks. These Vatican marks have been filed under a special rule for governmental marks. That means that they are not registered, but remaining as pending applications, which nonetheless serve the purpose of blocking other possible marks. So when, for instance, an Austrian company tried to register "Pope Benedict Pretzel," there was already a mark in line. (Plus, the problem they would face that the name of a living individual cannot be registered without his consent.)

Then there are litigation storm clouds above Castel Gandolfo, in order to possibly stop the Church from using the name Pope Emeritus, who also happens to be a rapper in Oakland, California. If true (and it sounds too good to be), a trademark still would not give a monopoly on words. It only allows exclusive rights to sell your goods and services free from interference by a competitor who may confuse your customers or, in an extreme circumstance, tarnish your brand image or blow the distinction between you (as a source) and the new user. So there should be no immediate worry that we have to replace "Pope Emeritus" with a term like "The Cleric Formerly Known As Pope."

While many would no doubt like to see what would happen if the Vatican could take over marks such as "The Cardinals" for the Papal baseball team, or "Miracle Whip" as the official sandwich spread of Vatican City, or maybe even "Spirit Airlines" (a Pope's got to get around, after all), the reality is that even staid, formal symbols need protection.

Even governments and Popes want to stop others from using their trademarks. They may have myriad reasons. In some cases, they want the right to control all uses. In some cases, they want to protect a stream of funding. In some cases, they may want to preserve a certain dignity and facilitate their ability to stop offensive uses.

In the United States, we are fortunate that unfair, disparaging, or confusing uses all can be stopped, even absent any formal filings in the Trademark Office. The marks owned by the Vatican are a special type, filed under a very old provision of an international treaty (Article "6ter" of the Paris Convention for Intellectual Property Rights). Most nations follow the rule of "No Registration, No Right." Here, though registration is not so crucial, even a Papal portfolio is assisted by filing in the Trademark Office.

Introduction and Commentary

Names that are not famous can still have a huge impact on voter perception: Can a brand even make an unknown entity appealing? How intrigued were prospective voters with the name Barack Obama:

Presidential Debate of Another Kind: Would Barack Obama by Any Other Name Really Have Won the Nomination in 2008?

Oct 11, 2012

Forget Ryan-Biden. Here's a debate for you: Whose name has given them a bigger political advantage: Mitt Romney, or Barack Obama? Based on that test, I'm voting for the President.

Mitt Romney has a political heritage. His father, George Romney, was a Governor of the state of Michigan, and for several months was believed to be the front-running Republican candidate for President in 1968. Political name recognition is hard to underestimate. A candidate must break through the clutter of opponents and give voters a reason to pay attention. A famous name will do that. Political dynasties are nothing new in this country. The Randolphs of Virginia, the Adamses of Massachusetts, up to the Harrisons (William H., and Benjamin—his grandson), Roosevelt, Kennedy and Bush, another Cuomo running New York and a Brown in California (succeeding not just his dad, but himself!). Why is "name" so important?

Well, why is a name important for anything? A name creates an impression and sends a message. When a name is associated with past positive success, the candidate has an upper leg on an opponent. If the political heritage relates to a popular, or in the case of a name like Kennedy, a mythologized predecessor, the political as well as emotional boost can be exceptional.

Granted, it is not as if name is the only advantage of political heritage. A political family brings more to the table than just a name, of course. It brings a background in the "family business." A candidate from a family with no political pedigree does not get the benefit of all of the access to political ideas and people that a legacy candidate does. Connections provide—not just in politics, but in most endeavors from business to sports to entertainment—a big boost to success. Do ballplayers' sons tend to succeed just because of genetics? That may be a big part of it, but they also become comfortable seeing how things work in the big leagues and being around great ballplayers and celebrities. They are not intimidated. Familiarity breeds certain confidence.

But make no mistake about the value of a name. For Mitt Romney, following a famous political dad gave him some instant credibility when he entered politics. As in, "of course he's running for Governor; his father was a Governor." To certain generations, Romney was a well-known political name. While Mitt branched out into other areas for his success in academics and business, both his contacts and his name must be invaluable assets to him. At least the "Romney" part of the name. (One could argue that his success has been remarkable given, well, "MITT.")

What about the President's name? Here was a man who, at a very young age with a thin political heritage and resume—by traditional standards—was able early on to capture voters' imaginations and take his success all the way to the top. Say what you like about the state of America right now, the cliché still holds true—he is the most powerful man in the world. I believe that a big part of President Obama's appeal was that he was different. He had a different family background, a different racial background, a different political path, and a different name.

Would the media have been so entranced with the candidacy of this junior Senator from Illinois had he been named "Barry Smith"? I really doubt it. Barry Smith sounds ordinary; more of the same.

Not strong and powerful (apologies to all the real Barry Smiths out there—you're different). As many people know, the President was known as "Barry" for most of his formative years, up to his first year or two of college. Reports say that friends told him if he wanted to be taken seriously, he should use his given name, BARACK, which was proud and distinct, and captured his personal heritage as well.

Would Barry Obama have captivated people's attention as a new and different choice? Maybe more than Barry Smith (there I go again!), but nothing like Barack Obama. The name Barack Obama was totally new, and candidate Obama embraced the name and the idea that he did not look like the presidents on American currency, as he was fond of saying on the 2008 campaign trail.

Until the time of Jimmy Carter, presidents were referred to only by their full given names, including a middle name or initial. The Carter presidency changed that. He was rarely James Earl Carter, as Bill Clinton was usually Bill, and only—like all of us—William Jefferson Clinton when he was in trouble, like when he was being impeached or something. Barack Obama has not gone by "Barack Hussein Obama," and one may query whether he would have had a chance at victory if he'd used his full name from the outset. For most Americans, for instance, Hussein was reserved for Saddam. But if Barack Obama was not Barack Obama, I believe his candidacy would not have been able to distinguish itself enough to defeat another political name with huge clout—Clinton.

Now in 2012, of course, Barack Obama's name has acquired a "secondary meaning," as we say in trademark law. For most of us, the name means the President of the United States, together with all his policies, positions, successes, and failures. We associate the name with a huge basket of meanings. But we no longer give the uniqueness of his name a second thought. That was not the case back in 2007, when the early campaign had a candidate so new and different that even his name was far outside the mold—and which forced people to pay attention. Barry Smith—same person different name—sorry; I don't see it having worked out

PART IV

POLITICAL BRAND NAMES TAKE ON A LIFE OF THEIR OWN?

Introduction and Commentary

A political family showdown took place in the election campaign of 2012 when Mitt Romney, a former governor of Massachusetts and himself the son of a prominent former Governor, George Romney of Michigan, won the nomination for the Republican party against President Barack Obama. Romney's father was himself a presidential contender in the 1960s, and now his well-known son was facing off against a major political brand name.

President Obama had the interesting and unique situation where a landmark piece of legislation began to bear his personal name. When Congress passed and the president signed the Affordable Care Act, it was regularly dubbed "Obamacare." Was Romney fighting against the Obama political brand name for the man as well as the brand name for the Obama Administration's signature piece of eponymous legislation:

Obamacare—The Other Trial

Mar 28, 2012

The Supreme Court of the United States isn't the only place that "Obamacare" is on trial this week. We now know that the Obama campaign has adopted the word Obamacare as its own. Since the term Obamacare didn't originate with the President or his advisers, embracing the term now is sort of curious. To some, it is a little bit like Richard Nixon retiring to a yacht named Watergate after his 1974 resignation.

But what does the "Obamacare" name mean? That's on trial today as well. Obamacare may be a name given to a political program, but it certainly has all the traits of a trademark: one word that speaks volumes about the product. Obamacare might have been conceived a neutral term, but it certainly has been wielded liberally by the program's many critics. For the Obama team to adopt it as their own? You could imagine the discussions. How to best spin off the negative implications? Turn it into a positive one.

In the courtroom, if two sides are fighting over the right to use a name, they're typically trying to show that one side's use is going to confuse consumers, to the other side's detriment. What if the critics cry foul? Obamacare is supposed to be negative. The court comes along and turns it into a good thing.

This can change the whole meaning of the word, and with it, the significance and usage.

This reelection maneuver can start you wondering: why don't opposition parties do this more often? Everyone remembers when FDR tried to pack the Trademark Office with applications to register the words "New Deal." Maybe President Warren G. Harding could have tried to capitalize on the Teapot Dome scandal by using this name for the U.S. Capitol Rotunda. After the Bay of Pigs invasion, some of the Harvard boys in the Kennedy administration were worried. "You know, Mr. President, we are taking a nosedive in the polls because of this 'Bay of Pigs' thing." They could have given the term a little positive caché by renaming it a trendy barbecue spot on Capitol Hill—you guessed it—*Bay of Pigs*. Critics called Secretary of State Seward's acquisition of Alaska "Seward's Folly." The Secretary could have spun it a different way, perhaps by launching a variety stage show.

The possibilities are endless.

In reality, there are no real trademark rights in public policies. That does not mean that someone could not have coined the term Obamacare and sought to protect it for certain products. In theory, Obamacare could be somebody's property if applied to a product (or service) furnished in private industry. But here, it is not the case. Time will tell whether the goodwill associated with the term Obamacare benefits the President or not. In the next few months, when reviews start coming in, the campaign can talk about how Obamacare is helping to build a Great Society. Whoops.

Introduction and Commentary

Obamacare spawned trademark application filings by many private companies seeking registration for marks, which included the word "Obamacare." The Trademark Office rejected these applications, claiming in fact that those trademarks would falsely suggest endorsement or ownership by the president:

Healthcare.gov: Lots to be Confused About, but Does Anyone Really Care Who Owns 'Obamacare'?

Oct 28, 2013

Marilyn Tavenner may be testifying tomorrow about Obamacare and the disastrous launching of the Healthcare.gov website. Others are rapt, trying to figure out the identity of the woman whose image first adorned the home page. But the U.S. Patent and Trademark Office is mounting a campaign to refuse trademark rights to anyone seeking a trademark that includes the name "Obamacare."

They are wrong in thinking that any private enterprise using "Obamacare" will confuse the public into thinking that the President owned the mark or "approves of this message," as they say.

Not to suggest the Commerce Department is protecting the President. It's just the government attending to its everyday business. In this case, they are wrong.

The word "Obamacare" was used almost mockingly at first. The President's political opponents thought this moniker meant "Big Government," and connoted welfare out of control. But then, the President surprised them all by saying he kind of liked the name "Obamacare."

So when a government program is called "Obamacare," can the President stop people from using it because it suggests an association with, or approval by, the President?

Over the past several months, several trademark applications have been filed for "Obamacare." The applicants range from educational institutions to fervent opponents of the law. One controversial application was filed for "Destroy Obamacare" T-shirts. It featured the slogan surrounded by a stethoscope attached to a stick of dynamite. The New Orleans attorney who created that T-shirt was donating $2 from every $20 sale to the St. Jude's Children's Hospital in Memphis until the Government shutdown ended. "How Obamacare Works," a proposed TV talk show broadcast, was filed by a lawyer in Zionsville, Indiana.

The denial of trademarks linked to the President's name is nothing new. In 2007 the USPTO denied an application for the trademark "Obama bin Laden," citing laws barring "scandalous" trademarks, those that create "false associations," and other problems. In 2010, trademarks were denied for "Obama Bahama Pajamas," "Obama Pajama," and "Barack's Jocks Dress To The Left" for pajamas and briefs. The applicant tried, apparently unconvincingly, to assure the examiner that there was no connection between the marks and "the United States President Barack Hussein Obama II." During the last presidential campaign, the Obama campaign succeeded in temporarily blocking a Washington, D.C. vendor from using its "Rising Sun" logo on the grounds of copyright infringement.

What this would mean is that no one, with the exception of Barack Obama, can lay claim to the exclusive use of his name.

Is that the right result? Of course not. No one would think these things are approved or endorsed by the President. No one can claim exclusive rights in "Obamacare." And they can't use it in a way that misleads consumers into believing the products they sell are "official."

But the prohibition against falsely associating with a living individual is way too much form over little substance. "Obamacare" is a name the President himself has endorsed (or at least adopted). That is consent enough, as far as trademark law is concerned.

Introduction and Commentary

By the way, Barack Obama was not the first politician to come along with a unique name. Next to Obama, perhaps one of the most distinctive political powerhouse names of the last few decades was a four-letter word beginning with "N":

What in the Name of Newt?

May 2, 2012

There is this theory that a politician's name will help him get elected. Most of the time, the reasons are clear. Someone whose last name is Kennedy is going to get more media and voter attention than someone whose last name is unknown. So how to explain Newt Gingrich, which—let's face it—is one weird name?

Of course, Newt is backing out of the Republican campaign today after a long up-and-down fight. First, he was given no chance. Then he was the front runner. Then back down the ladder. But think about the Gingrich name. His name had gone from being a late-night joke when he entered the national political scene for the first time, to be a huge asset in his campaign. It's an example of all that a name can say and be in national politics.

A key attribute of a famous name is that it is rich with meaning. Say NEWT GINGRICH to someone, and you can instantly elicit a 100-word composition on what the name means to them. The lists will vary wildly, depending on someone's own politics. But the words NEWT GINGRICH are supercharged. Though they mean different things to different people, they definitely have meaning. That's what a trademark is all about.

Interestingly, like many politicians before him (including two of the past seven presidents, Bill Clinton and Gerald Ford), Gingrich's name at birth was not the same as the name under which he'd later achieve fame and success. Born Newton McPherson in 1943, he was adopted by his stepfather very early on and took his adoptive father's Gingrich surname. Would a somewhat less obscure name like Newton McPherson have garnered him the same attention as the stark Newt Gingrich moniker? Who knows? Maybe Mr. McPherson would not have captured the imagination in the same way as the alliterative Gingrich.

Our current president has one of the more unusual names in the history of the office (some would say most unique, but then what do you do about the 13th president, Millard Fillmore). In my view, the whole Obama-led political course change in America in 2008 was inextricably tied to his unique name. But that's for another day.

Today, the name Newt Gingrich means so many things that we're actually blinded by just how unusual the name is. The past two decades have infused this name with so much emotion and so many positions that no one can any longer see the name as just a name. But transport yourself back to the '80s. Imagine Gingrich is a freshman Congressman from Georgia. The first time you heard his name on the nightly news (that would be how you first heard his name in the early '80s), you probably would have turned to the person sitting in the room with you and said, "did he just say Knew Beenagrinch" or "what was that, Diphosphate Illyavitch"? Let us say it didn't flow off the tongue.

Imagine, if you can, running for office for the first time with a name like that. "I am Newton Leroy Gingrich, and I want to be your Congressman." You first have to hurdle the "what was that name?" before you even get to have the voter listen to your ideas. Names send messages. Different-sounding names are an obstacle, at first, to understanding. The force of Gingrich's ideas and personality obviously allowed him to prevail and succeed, up to the highest levels of government.

Then, as happens with names, the name and the meaning become one. So by the time Newt ran for president in 2012, a dozen years removed from public service (though still very much in the public eye), his name was a huge asset in starting a campaign. No one heard the name Newt Gingrich in 2012 and said, "what's that again"? Or if they did, it wasn't because they didn't know what a "Newt Gingrich" was. The name became emblematic of an overpowering point of view of America. That is the power of a trademark. It matters not if the name is for a product or for a person. A legacy of famous political family names—a Kennedy, a Bush, a Roosevelt, and Adams or even a Romney—will give a giant leg up to any candidate. The famous name provides instant access to the media, to attention, and to a level of credibility. The name's legacy carries forward meaning from past generations. Sometimes, like in the case of Newt Gingrich, the political legacy can even be from your own career.

Introduction and Commentary

Donald Trump had his own adventures with terms coined in the political arena. Sometimes, political terms are not names but slogans, which themselves can lead to disputes between political camps. Barack Obama had "Obamacare." In the election of 2016, Trump rival Sen. Ted Cruz of Texas tried to characterize Trump's behavior as a "Trumpertantrum." This provided a good lesson in what can and cannot be protected as a trademark, again applying equally to a political tag as well as to any new product.

Can Trump Trademark Ted Cruz's 'Trumpertantrum'?

Feb 5, 2016

One question that trademark lawyers hear all the time is, "they can't trademark that, can they?" Take the recent news about the "Trumpertantrum." Did Donald coin the term? Maybe not. But that does not mean he can't claim it as his own.

Trademarks are interesting in that way. You can own a trademark because you are the first to use it in connection with a particular product or service. Sometimes clients will see a competitor take a common English language word and try to say no one else can use it on their products. Let's say you come up with a mouse that looks like a rock. And you call it "The Rock." There's a tendency to think, "it looks like a rock, and a rock is a common object. No one can really claim the exclusive right to stop me from using the word 'Rock' on a mouse or any other electronic input device."

Answer: Sure, they can. It happens every day. Just think about how a few short decades ago, apples were most famous for their connection with the damnation of mankind. Now the word " Apple " means phones, tablets, laptops, and music. It is easy to understand that no one else can use that word. Because a trademark is not about creating a new name, it is about creating an association between a work (real or made-up) and a product.

It also is not important who created the word. (Who created the word "apple?") Trademarks protect association. So while the trademark owner is free to create her own word to sell a product, what allows legal protection is not if the word is made up or a dictionary term (that can come into play, but it's what we trademark lawyers love to call a "factor" and not the whole question). Someone can invent a word, but unless they are using it on a product or service, there is no trademark right.

What does that mean for Donald Trump? It means that even if Ted Cruz made up the word "Trumpertantrum," Trump can still own the trademark for certain goods or services, as long as he is selling something with that word. Trademark rights cannot be owned in words. They can only be owned for words as used to identify a product or service, or a trait of that product or service.

There are exceptions, of course. What would the law be without exceptions? Let's say you want to jump on the "Trumpertantrum" term—which you did not create—to sell boxing gloves. According to the concept of first use—the first to use a name on a product has superior trademark rights—you should be able to legally sell "Trumpertantrum" boxing gloves, even though you did not coin the term. Ted Cruz, who seems to have invented the word, would have little legal basis to stop you, even as the "inventor" of the word. So far, so good. But what if you were Donald Trump and you said: "People seeing my name on these gloves will naturally believe that I make or endorse this product. They will be confused."

Even if the dispute is in Iowa, Trump wins. Because your right to take a word that you did not invent and apply it as a trademark is only allowed until that use would be likely to cause consumer confusion. Here, because the consumer might reasonably think that Trump owns or endorses any "Trumpertantrum" products or services, he can stop their use.

Think about this like "Obamacare." Certainly, the president didn't make it up. For a time, it was used derisively by critics of the plan. But, eventually, the president came out and said he actually liked the name, and it has stuck.

What if Ted Cruz says that consumers will believe any Donald Trump product sold under "Trumpertantrum" must be endorsed by Cruz? He's free to make that argument; if he can prove it, he can win. But Trump has a bit of a head start on trademark use.

In most trademark disputes, you can't go too wrong by asking yourself, "What do I think consumers would believe?"

Introduction and Commentary

A fascinating little story evolved from what turned out to be a flash in the pan of a phrase. A woman claimed that Ted Cruz stole "Trumpertantrum" from her:

Woman Says Ted Cruz is a 'Liar And A Thief' for Stealing Credit for 'Trumpertantrum'

Feb 7, 2016

OK, so forget about whether Trump or Cruz could protect the term "Trumpertantrum." Forget about whether it is a trademark at all.

A woman who describes herself as a "simple housewife in Baltimore with two disabled daughters" says that Cruz is a "liar and a thief" for stealing credit for coining "Trumper Tantrum."

Susan Tannenholz is livid. Here is what she says:

> I posted my original phrase on CNN's Wolf Blitzer's *The Situation Room* Facebook page on Wednesday, Feb 3rd, at 12:59 pm. I wrote "A typical 'Trumper Tantrum'" (by Susan Schwartz Tanenholz) as a comment to *The Situation Room's* story, "Donald Trump accuses Ted Cruz of stealing Iowa Caucus..." Well, it looks like Ted Cruz stole again (LOL), but this time from me.
>
> I also posted that I had coined this new phrase to my very own Facebook page earlier on Wednesday, Feb 3rd, at 12:12 pm.
>
> Then four hours later, it's ALL OVER CNN! And Ted Cruz has claimed it as his own! Apparently, Ted Cruz (or one

of his staff members) read CNN's "The Situation Room's" article, and LOVED/STOLE my phrase "Trumper Tantrum"!

So, If Donald Trump wants to Trademark 'Trumper Tantrum,' perhaps you can forward him my contact info."

At the end of the day, none of this changes the "Trademark" status of this term. Regardless of who gets credit for inventing this phrase, it only becomes a trademark if and when it is used to sell goods or services.

As for Ted Cruz: he may be evangelical, but he was not the Creator of "Trumpertantrum."

Introduction and Commentary

Name recognition and brand protection. They go together. Even for ex-politicians. Let's turn to the example of former Minnesota Gov. Jesse Ventura, in the following piece written right after Jesse Ventura prevailed in a defamation lawsuit:

Jesse Ventura Lawsuit: Brand Protected!

July 30, 2014

What does the "Jesse Ventura" brand represent? It proves, even by the celebrity's own admission, that his brand is all about his reputation, and since it is a personal brand, about Jesse Ventura—the person.

Jesse Ventura just won almost $2 million in court in a defamation suit. He is quoted in the Minneapolis Star Tribune as saying that if he lost the case, he would have "permanently moved to Mexico." In the ex-governor's words, "If you can't win in court with the truth, there's nothing left." If this is not the Jesse Ventura brand, I don't know what is.

Ventura's career has shown how with the right mix of personal appeal and personal branding, a Navy SEAL turned professional wrestler can become governor. He's hardly the first celebrity to succeed in politics. But his brand, more than almost any other, keeps being reinvented.

The national media looked at his candidacy as a joke when he ran for governor of the State of Minnesota in 1998. But when he won the election, he won a lot of fans in the process. The image of a Navy SEAL may play well in any political race. The image of a pro wrestler? Probably not so much.

Since his time in the Minnesota State Capitol, he has been a media celebrity doing all the celebrity things that are customary in today's media. The defamation story accuser (attributing to Ventura anti-American, anti-military sentiments) hit at the center of the Ventura brand. It is like saying Ronald McDonald is actually a pitchman for Taco Bell (oh, wait). But really, our politicians chase after name recognition. Votes are largely about trust. People feel they trust names that they have heard of, and are far less likely to endorse names they don't recognize. The "Jesse Ventura" trademark has a very long tail, and with the proper care and feeding, names like this can sustain a long career.

Like with a product, the name must generally have something to back it. Take away his enormous size (six-foot-four, 255 pounds) and WWF history, and you are still left with a glossy reputation for brash outspokenness. Love it or hate it; there is a message to "Ventura"—a brand. His name got him attention, even if only as a sort of "shock value," which gets people to pay attention to him. But then, like the brand, he must deliver.

This lawsuit would have been different, and in fact, likely would not have existed, if Ventura were a relative unknown. Commentators today are marveling at how a man who was such a high-profile athlete/politician/celebrity/entertainer, and who therefore was a legitimate target for all sorts of public accusations, could win this case. Jesse fought to restore his brand, which is what he called his good name and won. No need to move to Mexico (spoiler alert: the newspaper report did note that he already has a house there, and spends the long Minnesota winters in the Baja sunshine). The Ventura brand can stay All-American.

Introduction and Commentary

Even some of the most famous and iconic brands fail. Sometimes an iconic brand alone cannot keep a company with other, less successful products, afloat. Big-name brands have ended up in the trademark graveyard. But sometimes, trademarks are snatched from the grave before their accrued goodwill grows cold. These brands, resuscitated by investors, make the graveyard more like a trademark limbo than a final resting place. There is just too much potential goodwill left in those names to let them stay buried forever. The significance of a product, service, or person's good name does not vanish all at once. It only evaporates over time. That period of time is measured not in months but in years, and once in a while even in decades:

Hostess with the Most-est? No Wonder That These Twinkies Will Not Join the Trademark Graveyard

Nov 16, 2012

The news today is that Hostess Brands is shutting its doors. As we all know, Hostess created iconic brands like TWINKIES, DING DONGS, WONDER BREAD, and of course, HOSTESS CUPCAKES. After 75 years, Hostess is succumbing, unable to restructure under the provisions of the bankruptcy code, done in by a labor dispute which Hostess says finally forced its hand.

When I think of Hostess, I think of kids.

TWINKIES is a product that conveys so much meaning, a name often used derisively as the standard-bearer for things that taste good (or at least we remembered it that way) but were not exactly vitamin- or nutrient-laden. What about WONDER BREAD? To my generation, any bread which could build strong bodies—let alone one that could do it 12 ways—had to be impressive. It should have been bulletproof, virtually the nectar of the gods. Speaking personally, I never have had a slice of Wonder Bread in my life; but still, I can relate.

Then there is the HOSTESS CUPCAKE (the chocolate ones, those I've had) and its fantastically imaginative offshoot, the pink

HOSTESS SNO BALL. If ever we have found a more rich concoction of chemical, color, packaging, and imagery, I don't know where it would have been. These names, these brands, speak volumes to generations of consumers.

Ironically, in our chronically obese culture, one reason that Hostess gives for failing is the decline in sales of traditional junk food brands. But really? Some of the most dominant brands in the United States are things like COCA-COLA, PEPSI, DORITOS, TOSTITOS, and as many brands of potato chips as you could care to list. These very literally fill the aisles (and many end caps) of every supermarket and superstore in the country. I don't know if snack foods differ so much from so-called "junk food;" probably junk food manufacturers don't think that's such a great category name for their offerings, and prefer something a bit less judgmental. Perhaps.

An interesting phenomenon in the fiercely advertised and promoted junk food and "salty snack" category is that potato chips, of all things, seem to have a healthy competition going, which includes many store and regional brands. I don't know how the local products' market share fares versus 20 or 30 years ago, probably not great. But there seems to be something about this product that lends itself to local loyalties, despite massive national advertising onslaughts.

So how is it that truly famous brands like those of Hostess can't keep pace anymore in today's marketplace? The brands are strong ones. Could it be that they are strong only to those of a certain generation who no longer are quite as avid consumers of their products? The images I have for these products are very much as kids' snacks and kids' food (build strong bodies). Maybe Hostess didn't keep up with advertising to a relevant consumer anymore.

People are talking a lot more today about healthy eating, that's for sure. Schools talk about—and in many cases are—ridding themselves of certain candy and soda offerings. So if today's kids can't find TWINKIES in the cafeteria, they would have to go and find these contraband things the old fashioned way—on the streets. But on the streets, other junk food must have a much higher profile.

David Letterman, a voice of the Baby Boom, reminisced earlier this week. He described the mystery of how the inside of the TWINKIES cellophane bag always managed to stay sort of damp and fogged up. But he also implied that nothing ever tasted better.

Hostess is, unfortunately, more than a brand for its 18,500 employees in 33 locations across the country who will be without jobs, just ahead of the holiday season. A Thursday evening deadline came and went without a deal. This morning, Hostess attorneys went into court seeking permission to end operations at its factories.

However, memories of those squishable loaves of WONDER-BREAD and sugar-caked fruit pies are etched in the collective consciousness of Baby Boomers across the country. What about the goodwill locked up in those names? It would seem unlikely that the Hostess portfolio will join a list of iconic brands in the corporate "Trademark Graveyard." In the business cycle, we always lose brand names: Panama no longer flies, though there has been more than one attempt to re-launch it. Polaroid cameras, Texaco petroleum, and Zenith electronics are among the many which once held prominent places in the pantheon of American business. Mergers, acquisitions, bankruptcies, and the march of technology have subsequently sidelined all of them. But these fates are not inevitable. Consider the almost astounding number of brands that flourish not just year after year, but decade after decade: DIAL soap, TIDE detergent, CREST toothpaste, OREO cookies, and LAND O'LAKES butter were category leaders a half-century ago, and even before. Guess what? Names like these have legs.

It would be hard to believe that someone won't pick up these Hostess brands and re-launch most of them. This may not be your grandfather's "white bread" America any longer, but it would be hard to imagine that someone can't put a lot of these Hostess names on products and make some good money. TWINKIES ICE CREAM, anyone?

The only name of the group that may not excite anyone is the company name itself: HOSTESS. Maybe it seems a bit outdated and tired. And truly, has anyone ever had a real grown-up hostess serve them TWINKIES for dessert?

Introduction and Commentary

Like any good brand, the "Trump" brand can be expanded to new lines and new subsidiaries. Enter "Ivanka":

The Four Lessons of Ivanka Trump (the Trademark)

Jul 25, 2018

When I heard that they were shutting down the "Ivanka Trump" brand, I wondered what broader lessons could be learned from this decision about trademark law. The big picture is simple. A famous name will sell lots of goods. Whether it can be done profitably is always another question. And a product that lives by the brand's recognition might die when the brand is tarnished.

How many entrepreneurs are there in the clothing and accessories business who have great new creations, an innovative brand, and unique marketing? All packaged up and represented by a great trademark? But people will not hear your great name without advertising, without lots of social media, influencers, and good old fashioned word-of-mouth; even a great brand name will not, by itself, save a product. It is a fact of business life that someone else may have a far inferior product (and I am not saying Ivanka Trump has been that), but will sell a ton of products if the brand name is already known.

So lesson one is: sweat the details to come up with a great trademark. But do not be quick to confuse your great brand—a name that encapsulates your whole product—with being the whole key to a successful product.

A mundane but already household-name trademark will beat your creative startup almost every time.

Lesson two, which therefore flows from this: do not fall in love with your killer brand name for a new product. Time after time (after time), I have seen a company try everything it can to find a way to make a bad name (more on that in a second) viable. A bad trademark can be one which so totally describes the product that you cannot stop others from using the same word. "The Chair" may project confidence and a desired sense of arrogance for a boldly styled chair. But you will never be able to stop imitators from using your name when they copy your successful idea. Or maybe (this is very often the case) you will have a mark which is similar to one or more trademarks already in use.

Your lawyer says it is going to lead to problems, but you just *know* this mark is the one and only. It is not. A name that you cannot protect or which will only lead to a lawsuit is not a great asset. A great, strong name like "Ivanka Trump" can sell anything (or sell it at least once, even if the quality is subpar). A great trademark will not assure a successful product in most cases. Be passionate about your mark, but not fanatical. Know when to say "when."

From what I read, it seems that Ivanka was still drawing a nice seven-figure salary from the company, but, of course, it is never assured that a high CEO salary equates to profitability. In any case, factors outside one's direct control can cause a brand to tank. Putting aside the discussion of whether Ivanka could have chosen between her clothing line and her West Wing office, bad press about the brand (even if not the product) can become impossible to overcome.

This leads to lesson three: if your product has been successful, be careful where and how you extend it.

Damage to the brand on any product can have a huge impact on everything else in the product line. Consumers see a brand as having a single image, often regardless of the product. I know many people are thinking, "we should be so lucky." But that is not completely true. A "version 3.0" rushed to market can damage the reputation of the trademark. A trademark is an indication of origin (which a bad extension will kill) and designation of a certain quality (ditto).

Damage those indicators, and you damage your mark, and that may make it hard to enforce against an infringer down the road. There is not a lot of trademark precedent for tracking damage to a brand when the owner is the *Leader of the Free World*, and the trademark can take a hit because of North Korea, Iran, or Russia. Trademarks have been tarnished by a person's dumb tweet, or in earlier times, by a stray statement quoted in a trade magazine.

There is at least one more fourth lesson: it is very difficult to measure the significance of the trademark on a product's success. In litigation, it is so difficult that owners of multi-million (or even multi-billion) dollar brands hire survey experts to measure all sorts of things about what the brand means, to whom, and whether consumers will be confused between it and another brand. So, if you struggle to assess the impact of your brand name of your new product or business, you are not alone. If global brands need experts to assess trademark impact, it may be that your gut instinct as an owner close to the business may be a strong substitute.

Forbes' recent cover story about Kylie Jenner and the top-earning women in business called Jenner a person with virtually no employees, capital, or expertise. Ms. Trump has some (but not many) employees, certainly has capital, and it is hard to say whether she brought true expertise to her clothing endeavor. But what was described as a "new model of extreme fame leverage" can put a trademark on a roller coaster ride that few brands have ever seen in our commercial history.

The lessons above find a common theme all brand owners can heed. But on the other hand, these celebrity trademarks now appear to exist in their own universe.

Introduction and Commentary

Laundry detergent, ground coffee, beer, or political families—all brands tend to follow almost the same patterns and rules as they grow in significance and in value. They generally succeed or fail for largely the same reasons. Political symbols are not immune to these general trademark concepts. Take the idea of an elephant representing the Republican Party:

Memo to Republican Convention: Unless Chris Christie is Going to be Your Nominee, Ditch the Elephant!

Aug 28, 2012

Why is a convention a convention? No, not a capital "C" Convention. What I mean is, why has it become "conventional" for the Republicans to be represented by an elephant? And the Democrats by a donkey? Those names and symbols dig down deep—deep—deep into our political mindsets. Names are important everywhere, no more so than in American politics.

I quickly researched to find the answer to that question. I turned first to two other venerated and relatively well-known names. I checked out the *Encyclopedia Britannica* and the *World Book Encyclopedia*. I said I turned to them, not that they supplied my answers. Since those professionally edited and authoritative collections require a subscription, and since I don't have one, I went to the place I planned to go initially: *Wikipedia*, which tells me that the elephant was first publicized in a Thomas Nast cartoon in the 1870s, though not explaining WHY an elephant. Wikipedia shared a bit more about the Democrat's donkey, pointing out this has never been fully adopted by the party. It is said to come from criticism of President Jackson, whose opponents labeled him a "jackass."

Some states and regions have used other symbols over the years for the major parties, but none of us really recognize anything but the elephant and donkey.

Names often evoke strong images. How many people who are dreaming up names violently reject choices based on their emotional reaction not to the sound of the name but to the connotation? The answer is that almost everyone has done that (unless your name is Thurston Howell II, in which case your son's name is pretty well decided already).

In reality, there are precious few names that objectively have any undesirable traits. Traits are tacked on by our personal interactions and observations of people with a particular name. Take the top 10 girls' names according to the Social Security Administration in May 2012. When I was a kid, Sophia, Emma, Olivia, Ava, and Emily (respectively numbers 1, 3, 4, 5, and 6) all were "old lady" names. Say "Emily" to me when I was twelve, and I'd picture a very thin, frail, little old lady with a shawl. Olivia was more or less the same, give or take five pounds. Isabella and Mia (2 and 9) just weren't around; if you ever heard them, they were very ethnic names, someone's older immigrant aunt with a babushka.

Abigail (7) was around a bit—and everyone knew it was a very cool name [note: my 18-year-old daughter is Abigail]. Madison (8) was an avenue, a president, or a city. Never a name. The tenth most popular name—Chloe—you just never heard and literally would not know how to pronounce. I first heard it when I owned a couple of retail stores, where we sold CHLOE perfume back in the early 80s.

Thirty years ago, if you told your friends and family that you planned to name your daughter most of these names, they would be all over you, and tell you why those were just bad names. "How could you do that to a little baby?" OK, Igor is not the nicest sounding name, and Penelope is always going to sound like a fruit. But like in many things, there is a simple rule to explain how things work. In real estate, it's location, location, location. In names, it's all association, association, association.

The Republicans are spending about $73 million to put on this convention (exclusive of rainwear). Image is everything in politics these days (unless you're one of those who count the issues as important). Mitt Romney is already basically a household name in America. Still, he'll spend about a billion dollars to get his name out in front of the voters. Barak Obama is already a household name around the world. He'll spend about a billion, too. So, with all this money flying around, why is no one at GOP headquarters trying to spend on a trademark and come up with a better symbol than an elephant? I'm not talking about tweaking the artwork, as they do every now and again. I'm talking about a new symbol.

What does the elephant symbolize? What does it tell voters? Candidates are not packaged products that people are going to buy because they trust the elephant brand on the label. To mix a metaphor, the elephant is the cart pulling the horse. People know "Republican," and say, "Oh yeah, they have the elephant." Let's see. An elephant is slow. Check. They tend to live longer (60-ish) than most mammals except for us, and even the babies look wrinkly. So they're old. Check. They're reputed to have long memories. So they carry a grudge. Got it. We associate them with a circus. Excellent. They are not associated with wisdom (owl), courage (lion), or national affiliation (eagle).

C'mon people. If politics is marketing, let's market already. Since this is the Republican's week, I'm focusing on them. The Democrats will have their own chance to turn away from the donkey, the connotations of which are so bad that you can't even comment. How about a symbol or a logo that neither stinks like an old animal nor looks like it was created in a middle school graphics art class (have you seen the logo the Dems are using in Charlotte)?

Tonight's keynote speaker is New Jersey Governor Christie. He talks about his weight but does not seem to disclose it. About a year ago, the *New Republic* took an informal reader poll and arrived at 334 pounds. The only man to rival that size in the oval office was

President Taft, who may have tipped the scales at 340. He was a Republican, but don't blame him. The elephant was long entrenched before he gained office.

CONCLUSION

For centuries, people have relied on simple names for reassurance.

Brand names are just about the most efficient means of communication humans ever have developed. Brand names are like the infinitely dense particles of the Big Bang that explode and expand with meaning as time goes on. As long as there continue to be elements to fuel growth and so long as the brand name neither breaks its promise nor loses its relevance over time, it will continue to perform in almost miraculous ways.

A single word—or just one phrase—can encapsulate years or decades of history and convey meaning that even a thousand words could not begin to capture. A brand name—a trademark—helps people know what to buy, who to trust, who to hire, and even guides voters to an Election Day decision.

No one has ever doubted that "TRUMP" is a brand. Exploiting fame for political reasons is not unique to Donald Trump, as many otherwise have crossed over from entertainment (Ventura and Reagan, for instance) to politics. The "TRUMP" brand has both a business image (Real Estate properties) and an entertainment one. But these commercial brands, and then eventually his political brand, all behave as political brands have before him, and as commercial brands always have.

At first, major concerns were expressed about whether Trump would in fact continue to actively try to exploit the White House for the exposure it would bring to his commercial brand. There was also speculation about whether he (or the "IVANKA TRUMP" brands) would develop new Trump properties during his time in office. These concerns appear to have settled down, as the organization continues to operate under the supervision of sons Eric Trump and Donald Trump Jr., while the overt exploitation of the presidential pulpit to grow commercial brands has not been as prevalent as perhaps some people feared.

This is not to say that there were not complaints about potential conflicts which flowed from benefits the Trump Organization stood to gain in its businesses. There have been reports about housing U.S. security and military personnel, and even the vice president at Mr. Trump's Irish or Scottish properties, or other plans to host world leaders at Trump properties when they attended international conferences, Although the U.S. economy grew stronger month by month during the Trump presidency until the COVID pandemic, there was little outward evidence of ongoing active exploitation of the "TRUMP" trademark spring-boarding from Donald Trump's notoriety and fame as President of the United States.

At one point, early in the Trump presidency, there was talk about a moderate-priced hotel chain. Who knows if that might come to fruition? The "TRUMP" name has long been associated with bigger resort and luxury properties, golf courses, apartments and office facilities, so there is no reason to believe that branding will not continue in the future, with the "TRUMP" brand's degree of notoriety multiplied countless times over as a result of Donald Trump's time in office.

The American public has tended, almost uniformly, to treat former presidents with great respect, deference and even affection. Donald Trump has a different profile; whenever he leaves the White House, whether in 2021 or 2025, will he be treated with that same traditional public admiration and enter a retirement mode as an elder statesman? That remains to be seen. It is not unreasonable to expect that he and his organization will fully exploit all of the fame that has accumulated in order to enhance the commercial side of the "TRUMP" brand in United States, and around the world.

The question is: how will the brand act in the future? Donald Trump's name has been spoken, featured, displayed, criticized, reviled, praised, and venerated. In one context or another, "TRUMP" has, in the U.S.A. alone, been repeated in mainstream media thousands or tens of thousands of times each and every day. His exposure has probably been almost as great in foreign countries. There is no reason why the adage that "it does not matter *what* they say as long as they spell your name right" will not fully apply to the "TRUMP" brand in the future. It will not be surprising to see tremendous exploitation of the brand in Mr. Trump's post-presidential era. The possibilities would seem to be considerable. Whenever Donald Trump leaves office, the brand will seem to be ripe for Donald Trump's future political exploitation by Mr. Trump himself, by Ivanka, or his other children. The "TRUMP" name will also be well positioned for selling products and services to what—at an absolute minimum—will be a core base of supporters, numbering in the tens of millions. The political brand and commercial brand will merge in a way with little precedent in U.S. commercial and presidential history.

For politicians as products, "brand names" means name recognition, which helps people believe they are avoiding the risks of the unknown. Perhaps because the "purchase" of a political candidate is less frequent than, say, a bar of Ivory soap, a consumer's trust in a political brand name, at least for the candidate's first election for any office, is still a gamble. Ivory soap built its reputation on being 99 44/100% pure. That original claim to fame has long since disappeared from most products carrying the Ivory brand. Does the promise of purity remain?

***

For more about this, keep your eyes out for my new book, *Brand Names and Politics*, set to be released in December 2020, which explores the rich history of brand names and political families, and their political dynasties. At the same time, we see why and how brands are successful, and why the principals—not just for the TRUMPs of the world—but for most political families, still follow the course of a good product brand.

CPSIA information can be obtained
at www.ICGtesting.com
Printed in the USA
LVHW021158301020
670162LV00004B/132